SPIDERS

by Jane Dallinger

Photographs by Satoshi Kuribayashi

A Lerner Natural Science Book

Lerner Publications Company • Minnea

Sylvia A. Johnson, Series Editor

Translation by Joe and Hiroko McDermott

The publisher wishes to thank Jerry W. Heaps,
Department of Entomology, University of Minnesota,
for his assistance in the preparation of this book.

LIBRARY OF CONGRESS CATALOGING IN PUBLICATION DATA

Dallinger, Jane.
  Spiders.

  (A Lerner natural science book)
  Adapted from The spider's secret by S. Kuribayashi,
originally published under title: Kumo no himitsu.
  Includes index.
  SUMMARY: Text and photographs describe how a
variety of spiders produce silk and use it for making
webs, trapping insects for food, and for other purposes.

  1. Spiders—Juvenile literature. [1. Spiders. 2. Spider
webs] I. Kuribayashi, Satoshi, 1939- II. Kuribayashi,
Satoshi, 1939- Kumo no himitsu. English. III. Title.
IV. Series: Lerner natural science book.

QL458.4.D34   595.4'4   80-27548
ISBN 0-8225-1456-7

This edition first published 1981 by Lerner Publications Company.
Revised text copyright © 1981 by Lerner Publications Company.
Photographs copyright © 1974 by Satoshi Kuribayashi.
Adapted from THE SPIDER'S SECRET copyright © 1974 by
Satoshi Kuribayashi. English language rights arranged by
Japan UNI Agency, Inc. for Akane Shobo Publishers, Tokyo.

International Standard Book Number: 0-8225-1456-7
Library of Congress Catalog Card Number: 80-27548

6 7 8 9 10 90 89 88 87 86 85 84 83 82

A Note on Scientific Classification

The animals in this book are sometimes called by their scientific names as well as by their common English names. These scientific names are part of the system of **classification**, which is used by scientists all over the world. Classification is a method of showing how different animals (and plants) are related to each other. Animals that are alike are grouped together and given the same scientific name.

Those animals that are very much like one another belong to the same **species** (SPEE-sheez). This is the basic group in the system of classification. An animal's species name is made up of two words in Latin or Greek. For example, the species name of the lion is *Panthera leo*. This scientific name is the same in all parts of the world, even though an animal may have many different common names.

The next group in scientific classification is the **genus** (GEE-nus). A genus is made up of more than one species. Animals that belong to the same genus are closely related but are not as much alike as the members of the same species. The lion belongs to the genus *Panthera*, along with its close relatives the leopard, *Panthera pardus*, the tiger, *Panthera tigris*, and the jaguar, *Panthera onca*. As you can see, the first part of the species name identifies the animal's genus.

Just as a genus is made up of several species, a **family** is made up of more than one genus. Animals that belong to the same family are generally similar but have some important differences. Lions, leopards, tigers, and jaguars all belong to the family Felidae, a group that also includes cheetahs and domestic cats.

Families of animals are parts of even larger groups in the system of classification. This system is a useful tool both for scientists and for people who want to learn about the world of nature.

Spiders can be found in gardens, fields, and forests all over the world. There are more than 30,000 different kinds of spiders, and all are able to make the special material known as silk.

Spiders belong to a group of animals that scientists call **arachnids*** (a-RACK-nids). Scorpions, daddy longlegs, and mites are also arachnids. They are some of the closest relatives of spiders.

Many people think that spiders are insects, but this is not true. There are important differences between spiders and insects. For example, spiders have eight legs, and insects have only six. A spider has two main parts to its body. An insect's body has three main parts. Many insects have wings, and most have feelers, or antennae (an-TEN-ee). Spiders have neither wings nor antennae. If you look carefully at spiders and such insects as ants or flies, you can see these differences.

*Words in **bold type** are defined in the glossary at the end of the book.

The drawing below shows you the different parts of a spider. The **cephalothorax** (sef-uh-leh-THOR-ax) is one of the two main parts of the spider's body. The legs are connected to this area. Inside the cephalothorax are **glands** that make poison. This area also includes the mouth, fangs, and eyes of a spider. Most spiders have eight eyes, although some have fewer.

The second main part of a spider's body is the abdomen. In the abdomen are glands that make liquid silk. After silk is made in the glands, it leaves the spider's body through **spinnerets** (spin-nur-ETS). Spinnerets are like small tubes. They lie at the back of the abdomen.

THE BODY OF A SPIDER

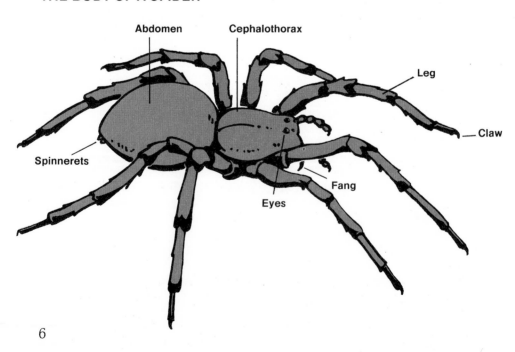

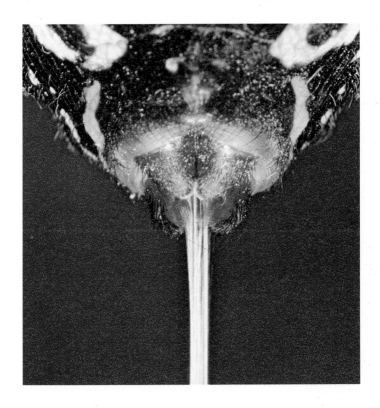

After silk passes through the spinnerets, it looks like just one thread. Actually, it has hundreds of fine threads in it. The threads stick together and form one thicker thread as they leave the spider's body. (The picture above shows silk thread coming out of a spider's spinnerets.)

Spiders make several kinds of silk. Most spiders have at least five silk glands, and the different types of glands produce different forms of silk. Some silk is sticky. Some is very strong and won't break easily. Each of the different kinds of silk has its own particular use.

7

Some silk is woven into webs to catch food. A garden spider of the genus *Argiope* made the web in the top picture.

Silk is also woven into nests. A comb-footed spider (*Theridion angulithorax*) used silk and sand to make the nest shown in the middle picture. The nest has been cut in half so that you can see inside it.

Spiders even use silk when they travel. The golden silk spider (genus *Nephila*) in the bottom picture is moving to a new home with the help of a silk thread.

There are many more uses for silk. Spiders weave it into special sacs to protect their eggs. It is used as a safety line to prevent spiders from falling. It can also mark a path so that a spider knows how to return home.

Many spiders use their silk threads to make webs. Spider webs are traps for catching insects, which are the **prey** of spiders. This means that insects are caught and eaten by spiders.

Each type of spider has its own way of spinning a web and its own web shape. One common type of web is the orb web (below). This web is fairly round in shape. Spiders that make orb webs are called orb weavers.

Orb weavers hide from enemies during the day. At night they become active, building webs to catch food. The pictures on the opposite page show an orb weaver making its web.

To begin, this spider goes to the top of a pole. It sends out some silk thread through its spinnerets. The wind carries the thread to a nearby roof. This thread becomes the bridge thread. It is suspended between the pole and the roof. The rest of the web will hang down from it. In picture #1, the red arrow points to a bridge thread.

Next, the spider goes back and forth over the bridge thread, spinning more silk to strengthen it. Then the spider begins to weave the rest of the web. It spins some radial (RAY-dee-uhl) threads, which go from the center of the web to the sides. In picture #2, arrows point to two radial threads.

The spider then begins to go in circles around the web, a short distance from the center. It spins some silk across the radial threads in a spiral pattern (picture #3). This area is a platform from which the spider can weave the outer part of the web. As the spider moves to the outer edges, it weaves a bigger spiral using a special, sticky silk (picture #4). At the same time, the spider removes some threads from the platform (picture #5). These threads may be wound into a ball and eaten. Finally, a completed orb web hangs from its bridge thread, ready to catch an insect (picture #6).

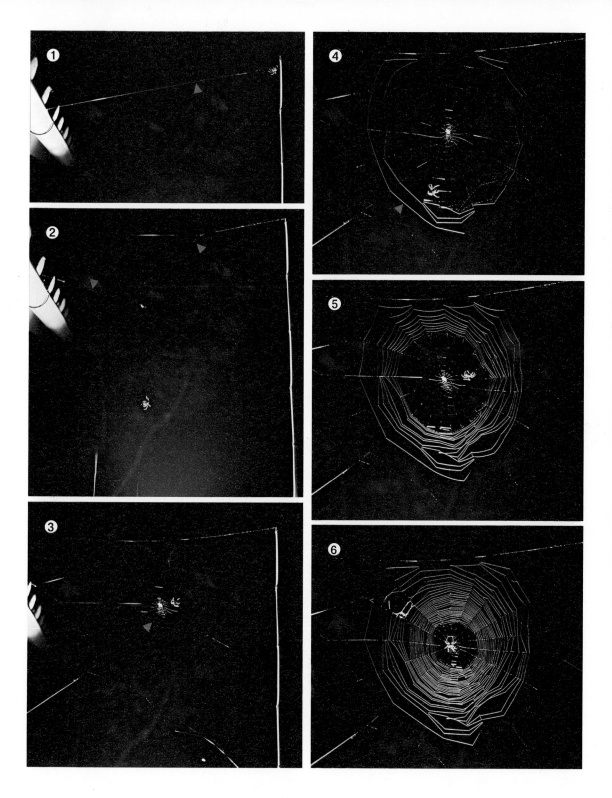

Some orb weavers make a new web every night. Others repair their old webs or replace parts of them.

After a spider finishes its web, it must hide. Otherwise, insects might see it and stay away from the web, or enemies might see it and attack. Some spiders leave their webs to hide nearby. Others weave special designs into their webs. When they sit quietly in the middle of these designs, they blend into the patterns and are hard to see. A garden spider is hiding in this manner in the picture on the left.

Different types of spiders make different designs to match the shape and color of their bodies. Another kind of garden spider blends into a different pattern in the picture on the right.

A hackled band spider (family Uloboridae) hides behind the design in its web (top). This spider lives at the center of its web most of the time. The design gives it very important protection from enemies. The ribbon-like material in the design is called a hackled band. The spider is named after this band. Silk threads are woven back and forth very close to each other to form the pattern.

Three-lobed spiders (genus *Cyclosa*) also spend most of their time on their webs. They use special material to make their designs (bottom). The patterns are made from the remains of insects caught by these spiders. Small twigs and other material may also be used.

In addition to orb webs, there are many other kinds of spider webs. For example, grass spiders (genus *Agelena*) build funnel webs in the grass or on low bushes. These spiders are also called funnel web spiders because of the shape of their webs.

The top part of the grass spider's web looks like a big sheet made of thread (left). The sheet serves as an insect trap. The bottom part of the web is a silk funnel (right). The funnel is a nest, and the spider lives in it. When an insect lands on the sheet, the spider comes up out of the funnel and grabs it.

In the picture on the opposite page, a small grass spider (*Agelena opulenta*) is attacking a young locust that has landed on its web.

A purse web looks like a long tube. To build this type of web, a purse web spider (genus *Atypus*) digs a hole in the ground using its long fangs (left). Half of the web is built in this hole and serves as a nest. The other half is built above ground with silk and dirt. It is attached to a rock or tree (right). The web may be 10 inches (25 centimeters) or more in length.

Insects become trapped on the top part of a purse web. The spider living in the bottom section rushes up to capture an insect as soon as it is trapped. The spider bites through the outside of the tube in order to reach its prey. Then it carries the insect down to the nest before eating it.

Many purse web spiders have attached their webs to these rocks.

Some comb-footed spiders (*Theridion angulithorax*) hang upside down inside bell-shaped webs (below). These webs are built in the cracks of rocks. They are made from sand and silk, and they also serve as nests. A close-up view of this type of web is shown in the middle picture on page 8.

The comb-footed spider is named for a comb of bristles on its fourth leg. The comb is used to wrap silk around insects that are caught in the web.

A spider of the family Urocteidae (above) makes a special web that has several layers of silk. This spider weaves its web in a tree or on the wall of a building. The web is thick and fairly small. It may be only 2 inches (5 centimeters) wide. The layers of silk in the web serve as a nest for the spider.

Many silk threads branch out from the nest area of this type of web. When an insect touches one of these threads, the spider feels the vibration in the line. The spider runs out to capture the insect (left) and then takes it back to the nest for a meal (right).

Most spiders that weave webs have poor eyesight. Their sense of touch tells them when an insect lands on the silk threads. A spider that lives on its web, like the spider shown on page 21, feels the threads shaking as soon as the insect touches them. It even knows the type of insect that has landed by the way the web vibrates.

A spider that doesn't live on its web feels the shaking through a **signal thread**. The signal thread goes from the spider back to the web. When a spider feels its web tremble, it moves toward its prey.

Some webs are made with sticky silk. They trap an insect as soon as it lands on the sticky threads. The more the insect struggles to escape, the more it becomes tangled in this type of web. Other webs are not sticky. When an insect lands on one of them, the spider must hurry to catch its prey before the insect can escape.

If a small insect is caught, the spider quickly pierces the captive with its fangs. Then the insect is carried home. If the captive is large, the spider first wraps it in more silk. This stops the insect from breaking lose or hurting the spider. The spider uses its legs to turn its prey around and around. As the insect turns, the spider covers it with newly spun silk.

Sometimes a trapped insect is too big for a spider to handle. Then the spider cuts some of the threads. The captive falls from the web to the ground and is free again.

Right: The garden spider spins its silk threads over the grasshopper.

Below: The garden spider turns the grasshopper around, completely covering it with silk. Next, the spider will cut the insect loose from the web and carry it home for a meal.

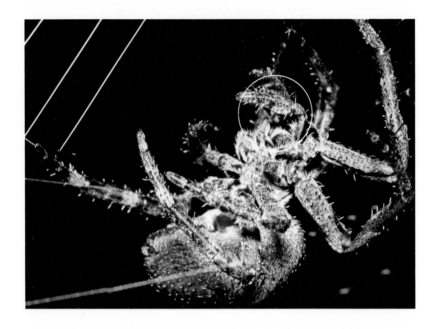

Spiders pierce their captives with sharp fangs as soon as possible. In the picture above, a white circle has been drawn around the fangs of an orb weaver (genus *Araneus*). On the opposite page, the orb weaver is sinking its fangs into a beetle. This sends a poison, or **venom** (VEH-num), into the beetle. Venom paralyzes insects and then turns their bodies into liquid. Spiders eat by sucking up the liquid.

The outer shells of some insect bodies are too hard for venom to dissolve. These shells are not eaten. Sometimes you can see them in old webs or spider nests.

Spider venom doesn't usually hurt humans. But black widow spiders (*Latrodectus mactans*) and a few others are poisonous to humans.

24

Not all spiders build webs. Many species use only speed and their deadly fangs to capture insects. The spider on the next page belongs to the family Liphistiidae. It lives in an underground burrow that has a door made of silk and dirt. The spider waits in the burrow, watching for insects through the partly open door (above). When an insect approaches, the spider leaps out and shoots venom into its prey with its fangs (opposite). Then the insect is taken into the burrow for the next meal.

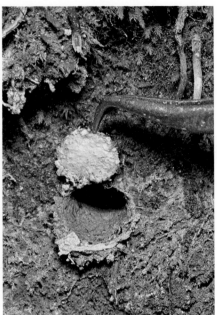

The silk-and-dirt doors to the underground burrows of spiders are called **trap doors**. Trap doors blend into the surrounding ground (above) and are difficult to see. This protects the spiders and their nests from enemies.

Another type of spider that lives in a burrow with a trap door is called the trap-door spider (family Ctenizidae). On the opposite page, a trap-door spider waits in its nest. The spider's burrow has been cut in half so that you can see inside of it. The open door is at the top of the picture.

Even though most spiders that live in burrows do not weave webs, they still spin silk. Some of their silk is used to build the trap doors. It is also used to line their nests and to protect their eggs.

Instead of building webs, jumping spiders (family Salticidae) use their excellent eyesight and jumping ability to catch food.

Unlike trap-door spiders, which wait for insects to approach, jumping spiders hunt for their next meal. These brightly colored spiders live in the grass or on trees. They are active during the day, moving around quietly as they look for food. When a jumping spider spots an insect, it spins a silk thread that serves as a safety line in case it misses its target. Then it makes a huge leap onto its prey. The jumping spider above (*Carrhotus detritus*) has just captured a fly in this manner.

Crab spiders (family Thomisidae) also catch food without using webs. They are named for their crab-like ability to walk backwards and sideways when necessary. Many of them hide in flowers. Insects that come to the flowers for a meal of nectar instead become the next meal for the waiting spider.

Color is very important to these spiders. Each type of crab spider is the same color as the flower it uses for its hunting ground. Because of this, it blends into its background and can't be easily seen by its enemies or prey.

The yellow crab spider (genus *Misumena*) on the left has just captured a drone fly. The white crab spider (genus *Xysticus*) on the right has surprised a bee that stopped for a drink of nectar.

A white crab spider (genus *Thomisus*) captures a bee.

Wolf spiders (family Lycosidae) also hunt for their food. These spiders are very common and can be seen in fields and among rocks. Some dig burrows, and others live under stones. Many wolf spiders live near ponds or marshes and catch insects that fly over the water.

Some spiders are so light that they can walk across water without sinking into it. Wolf spiders can walk on water for one or two steps between rocks or floating leaves. The wolf spider above (*Lycosa pseudannulata*) is carrying a dragonfly across a pond to its nest.

Wolf spiders would begin to sink if they tried to walk over a long stretch of water. Smaller hunters, such as nursery web spiders (family Pisauridae), can run across water for long distances without sinking.

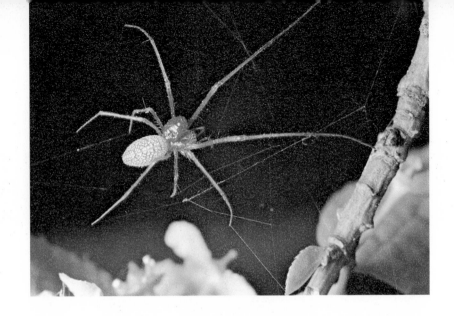

Spiders protect the balance of nature by eating insects. This keeps the insect population from growing too large. Nature's balance is also protected when spiders are eaten by such enemies as birds, toads, lizards, and monkeys.

Some enemies act as **parasites** (PAIR-uh-sights) on spiders. A parasite attaches itself to a spider and uses it as a source of food. For example, the parasitic red tick above is sucking the blood of a big-jawed spider (*Tetragnatha squamata*). Sometimes the spider remains alive and continues its normal activities while a parasite feeds on it.

Spider wasps are the worst enemies of spiders. A female wasp stings a spider, paralyzing it with venom (opposite). The wasp then digs a hole and puts the spider and one of her eggs in it. The egg develops into a young wasp that uses the spider for food. Some spiders remain alive for weeks in a paralyzed state until they are finally eaten.

Catching insects and hiding from enemies are two important parts of a spider's life. Another important part involves mating and laying eggs. Silk plays a major role in this. Some male spiders make special webs that are used during mating.

In the picture on the left, two golden silk spiders (genus *Nephila*) are getting ready to mate. The female is the bigger one of the pair. Female spiders are usually bigger than males.

After mating, female spiders lay their eggs on sheets of silk. Then they wrap the eggs in silk egg sacs, also called **cocoons** (kuh-KOONS). A cocoon protects the eggs as they grow. The picture on the opposite page shows the cocoon of a garden spider.

Some mother spiders leave once they lay their eggs and finish making their cocoons. Others stay to protect their cocoons. A mother may sit quietly and not even eat for days. She stays until the babies hatch from the eggs and then leave the cocoon. A female lynx spider (genus *Oxyopes*) is guarding her eggs in the picture above.

The cocoon of a female wolf spider becomes attached to her spinnerets (opposite). She carries it around with her. When the babies leave the cocoon, they climb on her back and ride with her until they can live on their own.

Left: **A female wolf spider carrying baby spiders on her back**

After hatching from eggs, baby spiders are called **spider-lings**. Some spiderlings stay in their cocoon for quite a while. Those that live in areas with long, cold winters may spend the entire winter inside their cocoon. Other spiderlings leave their cocoon soon after hatching.

As spiderlings grow, they shed their outer skin several times. This is called **molting**. The first molting actually occurs just before a baby spider leaves its egg. Once a spiderling hatches, it molts whenever it becomes too large for its skin. Most spiders stop molting when they become adults.

Spiders do not have soft skin. Instead, they have a hard outer covering that protects them. When a spiderling out-grows its skin, the covering splits apart. The spiderling then pushes its way out of the skin. A new, soft layer lies under the old one. After molting, the new skin hardens to form a protective cover once more.

Spiderlings also have the ability to grow a new leg if an old one is lost. When an enemy catches a spiderling or an adult spider by the leg, the captive can escape by breaking off its own leg. It then runs to safety using the other seven legs. A young spider will grow a new leg to replace the lost one. Older spiders can't grow new legs.

For a short time after leaving their cocoon, some spider-lings cooperate with each other. The orb weaver spiderlings on the opposite page worked together to weave a large web. They will all stay on that web for a day or two, until they can live on their own.

When spiderlings are ready to live on their own, many use the method of **ballooning** to find new homes. The spiderlings climb up blades of grass, branches, fence posts, or other objects. Then they spin some silk threads. (In the picture above, a golden silk spider is spinning ballooning threads.) When the wind blows against these threads, they float up like balloons, carrying the spiderlings into the air. Adult spiders also use ballooning to travel to new places.

The wind may carry ballooning spiders a short distance or many miles before they are able to land somewhere. The spiders then begin to build webs, dig burrows, or do whatever they must do to carry on life as adult spiders.

GLOSSARY

arachnids—the group of animals to which spiders belong. Other arachnids include scorpions, daddy longlegs, mites, and ticks.

ballooning—a method of travel used by spiders. When the wind blows against silk threads that are connected to a spider, the threads fly into the air and carry the spider up with them.

cephalothorax—the front part of a spider's body. It includes the head and chest areas.

cocoon—a sac made from silk by female spiders. It protects the spider eggs inside it.

glands—small organs in the body that make various substances. Spiders have some glands that make silk and others that produce venom.

molting—shedding the outer layer of skin. Spiders molt when they grow too large for their skins.

parasite—something that feeds and grows on a living organism without helping the organism in any way

prey—any creature that is hunted and caught for food

signal thread—a silk thread that goes from a hiding spider to the spider's web. When an insect lands on the web, the signal thread vibrates. This vibration serves as a signal to the spider. It tells the spider that something is in the web.

spiderling—the name given to a spider from the time it leaves its egg until it becomes an adult

spinnerets—small tubes at the back of a spider's abdomen. Silk passes through these tubes in order to leave the spider's body.

trap door—a door made by some of the spiders that live in burrows. It covers the top of the burrow.

venom—a poison that kills or paralyzes prey. Spiders inject their prey with venom by piercing captives with their fangs.

Left: Wet with dew, orb webs shine in the morning sun.

INDEX